A Bride's

The Honor Attendant

Hydrangea—devotion
White Rose—
gilrhood innocence

deserves a bouquet reflecting her meaningful place at the side of the bride. She is chosen to tend to the train and veil, hold the bridal bouquet while rings are given, and sign as a witness to the marriage. Married or maiden, she stands up for her sister or best friend on her wedding day.

Hydrangea & White Rose Bouquet:

12 white baby roses
5 or 6 blue and green hydrangeas
12 crystal sprays*
10 bead flowers
2 1/2 yards 1/2-inch-wide wired ribbon
1 1/2 yards 3/4-inch-wide wired sheer ribbon
21-gauge wire
vinyl tape
light green florist tape
corsage pin

Make this bouquet the day before the wedding.

Remove the leaves and thorns from the roses and wire the stems, then cover with florist tape. Using the florist tape, attach a crystal spray to each rose.

Gather the hydrangea flowers together, and arrange them in an oval bouquet, placing the green flowers on the bottom.

Thread the roses and the bead flowers through the hydrangeas.

Tape the stems together. Cut the stems across the bottom so they are even. Mist them well with water.

Put the bouquet in a container of water in a cool place.

Shortly before the wedding, remove the bouquet from the water, and dry the stems thoroughly.

Wrap the stems with the 1/2-inch-wide wired ribbon, and secure it with a corsage pin.

Double the remaining ribbon, and tie it securely around the handle at the top.

To finish, cut the streamers to varying lengths, then curl them around your fingers.

* easily found in crafts and florist supply stores

A Bride's Book

Organizer-Journal-Keepsake
for the year of the wedding

By Marsha Heckman
Photographs by Richard Jung

welcome
BOOKS

new york • san francisco

this book belongs to:

name: _____

address: _____

_____

phone: _____

Table of Contents

Published in 2007 by Welcome Books®
An imprint of Welcome Enterprises, Inc.
6 West 18th Street, New York, NY 10011
(212) 989-3200; Fax (212) 989-3205
www.welcomebooks.com

Designer: Lisa Vaughn/Two of Cups Design
Project Editor: Natasha Tabori Fried

ISBN 978-1-59962-042-8

Printed in China

SECOND EDITION

9   10

Introduction

From the time you decide to marry until your honeymoon you have about a million things to do to produce a perfect wedding. The organized bride has a budget, a detailed to-do list, and a calendar with all events and appointments faithfully recorded. You have contact and fitting information for each member of your wedding party, a record of all the vendors—the key people who provide services for the wedding—from the jeweler to the parking attendants. You need a file of guest information and a journal to record your feelings and memorable moments during this important time in your life.

A Bride's Book keeps all the resources and information at hand in one tidy place while you interview vendors, shop, or work. It is easy to use, with check boxes and expenditures listed on the outside margins for quick reference. It has tab dividers between each section, and an elastic band to keep the book neat. There are two pockets— one in front for brochures, bids, business cards, and receipts; another in the back for keepsakes—swatches, clippings, ribbon, invitations, notes, and cards.

A Bride's Book is illustrated with gorgeous photographs of some of my bridal bouquets. Each divider tells a story about these beautiful flowers and gives their meaning in the Victorian flower language. I have included a detailed "recipe" for the bride or sister or friend who wants to make the bouquet herself.

Your wedding plan evolves from the size, location, and the degree of formality you decide on. Your budget, your own style, and your fantasies of what your wedding day would be, define it. After you and your families have made these decisions, you begin to ask for referrals from married friends, attend wedding fairs, buy wedding books and magazines, conduct online research, and start making the all-important lists. Even the most organized couple can find this production overwhelming. The trick is to start as early as possible, get everything in writing, and keep it together in one handy place.

A Bride's Book will give you one organized place to keep all your wedding plans. It is convenient to carry, easy to use, and efficient. It is a treasured record to share with a friend and a beautiful keepsake of the time you spend planning and producing the event of a lifetime—your wedding.

To Do

Blue is the

Forget-Me-Not—
keepsake, love—pure and true

rarest color of flower. Blue flowers are planted in the garden especially to attract butterflies, bees, and birds. There is a story that in the Garden of Eden, when Adam had nearly finished naming all the animals and plants, one tiny unnoticed blue flower cried, "Forget me not," so he gave her that name. In another famous garden, Lady Chatterley's gamekeeper planted forget-me-nots between her thighs and declared, "There's forget-me-nots in the right place!"

Forget-Me-Not Bouquet:

48 forget-me-nots
6 to 8 large ivy leaves (about the size of your hand)
6 yards 1 1/2-inch-wide satin ribbon
a love letter
vinyl tape
dark green florist tape
21-gauge wire
corsage pin

This bouquet will look fresh if it is kept cool, so it can be made the day before the wedding.

The mushy stems of forget-me-nots are vulnerable and must be groomed with care. Carefully using scissors, remove all but the two leaves closest to each flower. As you work, separate the straight stems from the curved ones and keep the flowers in water.

Starting with the straight stemmed flowers, form a round bouquet. Tape the stems together. Add the curved stems around the outside edge, taping them in place as you work.

Cut the ribbon into 30-inch pieces. Make three loops in each piece of ribbon and secure it with a 10-inch piece of wire.

Using florist tape, attach one ivy leaf to each ribbon wire just beneath the bow.

Circle the bouquet with the wired bows, ivy leaves on the bottom, and tape them to the stems.

Cut the stems and wires straight across the bottom.

Roll the love letter into a small cylinder and tuck into bouquet.

To finish, wrap the handle with the remaining ribbon and secure it with a corsage pin. Keep in a cool place until the ceremony.

To Do

You can rely on this to-do list to navigate your way through the wedding process with efficiency, certainty, and little anxiety.

This list includes all the vital basics from ordering the dress and invitations, to choosing the flowers, booking the band or DJ, and writing your vows. The list reminds you to buy matching nail polish for the bridesmaids, make a new will, sign up for dance lessons, and spend 15 minutes alone with your parents before the ceremony. Start working on your list as soon as you know you are getting married. The best vendors and locations are booked well ahead of time, so the earlier you book, the better chance you will have of getting the key people you want.

When you have made the first essential decisions—formal or casual, big or small, hometown or destination wedding, the rest is just a long list of tasks to complete. Start searching for the location immediately. Many popular wedding sites are booked a year or more ahead of time. Try to be somewhat flexible about the wedding date and you may have a better chance of securing the place you want. Make appointments to interview the vendors as soon as possible. Look at their portfolios, get references (the best refer-ence is from a customer you know), and cost estimates in writing. There is a page for every service—caterer, musicians, photographer, florist, printer—and all the other key people who provide your wedding services.

Most bridal dresses are custom-made for you. The process from choosing your dress to the final fitting and delivery can take six months or more, so the sooner you find your perfect dress, the better. Begin by carefully reading the TO-DO list. If you follow this list faithfully, enter every appointment in the calendar section, then check off every task as you complete it, you can be assured no wedding detail will go unattended. Work together on the total budget figure and write estimates of what you think you will need to pay for services. Be flexible within your total. Some items may cost less than you expected. While others will cost more. Check off any tasks that do not apply to your wedding. Next, get started on the list and check the "complete" box when each activity is done. Don't hesitate to complete any task before its deadline whenever you can.

There "confirm" box is for the final weeks before the wedding when you confirm all arrangements and agreements. This will help relieve any anxiety you may have in the weeks before your wedding. When all the items on the to-do list are checked, you are ready for the big day.

· Budget ·

	BUDGET	FINAL COST

personal expenses

    engagement portrait

    wedding dress

    bride's wedding accessories & cosmetics

    bride's rehearsal attire

    bride's going-away attire

    honeymoon clothes

    doctor, dentist, blood tests, travel innoculations

    legal fees

    beauty services:

        massage

        facial

        manicure/pedicure

        hairdresser

        make-up artist

    groom's wedding attire

    groom's additional wardrobe

    wedding rings

    fiancee's gifts

    attendants' lunch or tea

    attendants' gifts

    gifts & ties for groomsmen

    dance lessons

ceremony

    wedding coordinator

    marriage license

· Budget ·

BUDGET	FINAL COST

printing:

   invitations, announcements, programs, etc.

   calligrapher

   postage

guest accommodations

transportation to & from ceremony

official's fee

wedding site fee

rentals for ceremony

ring pillow, unity candle

ceremony music or musician

flowers for ceremony site

wedding party flowers

rehearsal dinner

video

photographer

r e c e p t i o n

tent, lighting, etc.

reception site fee

flowers

music

parking valet

security

food

beverages

· Budget ·

	BUDGET	FINAL COST
service personnel		
rentals for reception		
favors		
toasting glasses, cake knife, guest book		
cake		
groom's cake		
favors		
after the wedding		
wedding night accommodations		
next day brunch		
honeymoon		
totals		

notes

_____

_____

_____

_____

_____

_____

_____

_____

· In the Beginning ·

COMPLETED   **CONFIRMED**

☐ ☐ arrange a meeting of your families to discuss possible dates, locations, size, & formality

☐ ☐ pick a date & back-up date

☐ ☐ make a wedding wish list together

☐ ☐ establish a budget

☐ ☐ discuss how you will manage your finances together

☐ ☐ request form for local newspaper announcement

☐ ☐ schedule engagement portrait

☐ ☐ start using your wedding organizer; write down ideas & recommendations

☐ ☐ choose your attendants

☐ ☐ collect vendor ads & brochures, pictures, wedding books, referrals from married friends & relatives

☐ ☐ conduct online research to generate ideas

☐ ☐ start shopping for the wedding dress

· Six Months to a Year ·

date: _____

	COMPLETED	CONFIRMED
prioritize your wish list	■	■
hire wedding consultant if you need help	■	■
start garden & fix-up projects for a wedding at home	■	■
make appointments to visit ceremony & reception sites	■	■
for a destination wedding, reserve site(s)	■	■
reserve blocks of rooms for guests	■	■
request hotel(s) information for guests	■	■
book hotels for wedding party & family	■	■
book ceremony location	■	■
book official(s)	■	■
sign up for any required class or counseling	■	■
order ketubah & yarmulkes, if necessary	■	■
book reception site	■	■
order wedding gown & headpiece & veil	■	■
give each member of the wedding party a contact list	■	■
choose your printer	■	■

date: _____

COMPLETED   **CONFIRMED**

☐   ☐   design invitation & "save the date" card

☐   ☐   order invitations & announcements, "save the date" cards, & note cards

☐   ☐   send announcement to newspaper(s)

make appointments to interview key people:

☐   ☐   caterer

☐   ☐   florist

☐   ☐   baker

☐   ☐   calligrapher

☐   ☐   photographer

☐   ☐   videographer

☐   ☐   band and/or dj

☐   ☐   ceremony musician(s)

☐   ☐   security service

☐   ☐   finalize guest list

☐   ☐   start compiling addresses

☐   ☐   ask families for their final guest lists

· Five Months ·

	COMPLETED	CONFIRMED
mail save the date cards	☐	☐
book key people:		
caterer	☐	☐
florist	☐	☐
calligrapher	☐	☐
photographer	☐	☐
videographer	☐	☐
band and/or dj	☐	☐
ceremony musician(s)	☐	☐
hairdresser	☐	☐
make-up artist	☐	☐
security service	☐	☐

· Four Months ·

date: _____

COMPLETED	CONFIRMED	
▪	▪	mail "save the date" card
▪	▪	choose favors, order
▪	▪	discuss honeymoon plans
▪	▪	sign up for dance lessons
▪	▪	order groom's tuxedo
▪	▪	order groomsmen tuxedos
▪	▪	order rings
▪	▪	order cake
▪	▪	choose attendants' gifts
▪	▪	choose fiancée's gift
▪	▪	shop for attendant dresses
▪	▪	shop for mother's dress & accessories
▪	▪	shop for trousseau & honeymoon clothes
▪	▪	engage parking valet service
▪	▪	apply for tent & parking permits
▪	▪	reserve rental items & tent

· Four Months ·

	COMPLETED	CONFIRMED
make wedding night reservations		
reserve hotel rooms & transportation for out-of-town guests		
arrange transportation for wedding day		
arrange transportation for rehearsal dinner		
book honeymoon tickets & lodging		
check on printing order delivery		
make appointments for medical exams		
make appointments for dental check-up		
sign up with gift registries, in stores & online		
create your personal wedding website		
renew passport		

date: _____

COMPLETED	CONFIRMED	
▪	▪	send envelopes & guest list to calligrapher
▪	▪	arrange rehearsal dinner (see page 25)
▪	▪	arrange day-after brunch (see page 26)
▪	▪	arrange babysitter for reception
▪	▪	schedule time to assemble favors
▪	▪	shop for bride & attendants' accessories, shoes, lingerie, jewelry, nail polish, & lipstick
▪	▪	buy guest book, toast glasses, cake knife, unity candle, & ring pillow
▪	▪	travel innoculations
▪	▪	execute new will
▪	▪	schedule massage and beauty treatments

· Six Weeks ·

	COMPLETED	CONFIRMED
mail invitations	■	■
discuss ceremony with official(s)	■	■
choose readings	■	■
choose readers	■	■
write vows	■	■
create the ceremony program	■	■
send ceremony program to printer	■	■
make itinerary of events & activities for destination or out-of-town guests	■	■
open bank accounts	■	■
blood tests	■	■

update official documents:

	COMPLETED	CONFIRMED
driver's license	■	■
social security	■	■
medical & life insurance	■	■
credit card applications	■	■
post office change-of-address	■	■

· One Month ·

date: _____

COMPLETED	CONFIRMED	
☐	☐	marriage license
☐	☐	address announcements
☐	☐	pick up rings
☐	☐	break in wedding shoes
☐	☐	make song list for band/dj
☐	☐	arrange seating plan
☐	☐	write thank-you notes as gifts arrive
		(this will save time later!)
☐	☐	assemble favors with attendants
☐	☐	finalize menu with caterer
☐	☐	invite attendants to lunch or tea
☐	☐	confirm transportation for rehearsal dinner & wedding day
☐	☐	confirm accommodations & transportation
		for out-of-town guests

· Two Weeks ·

date: _____

	COMPLETED	CONFIRMED
write itinerary for the wedding day & distribute copies to wedding party & vendors	▪	▪

confirm costs & review itinerary with key people:

	COMPLETED	CONFIRMED
florist	▪	▪
baker	▪	▪
photographer	▪	▪
videographer	▪	▪
band and/or dj	▪	▪
ceremony musician(s)	▪	▪
hairdresser	▪	▪
make-up artist	▪	▪
transportation	▪	▪
security service	▪	▪
travel agent	▪	▪
confirm final count with caterer	▪	▪
confirm rentals delivery	▪	▪
have a practice appointment with hairdresser	▪	▪
make-up practice appointment	▪	▪
have a final fitting & pick up wedding dress	▪	▪

· One Week ·

date: _____

COMPLETED   **CONFIRMED**

☐ ☐ review duties with wedding party

☐ ☐ assign helpers for wedding day (see page 86)

☐ ☐ give final place card list to calligrapher

☐ ☐ bridal attendants' party

☐ ☐ give gifts to your attendants

☐ ☐ indulge in beauty treatments

☐ ☐ pack for wedding night & honeymoon

☐ ☐ make a wedding day kit

☐ ☐ write toasts for rehearsal dinner & reception

☐ ☐ get travelers checks for your honeymoon;
        get foreign currency if necessary

☐ ☐ write checks to key people, give to best man
        to distribute

☐ ☐ finalize seating chart

☐ ☐ memorize your vows

· The Day before ·

date: _____

	COMPLETED	CONFIRMED
give helper unity candle & ring pillow to deliver to ceremony	■	■
give helper(s) place cards, favors, guest book, cake knife & server, & toasting glasses to deliver to reception site	■	■
check your dress & accessories	■	■
check your going-away outfit	■	■
have a massage	■	■
have a manicure/pedicure	■	■
practice your vows	■	■
rehearse the ceremony	■	■
take an hour to relax!	■	■
attend rehearsal dinner	■	■

· On Your Wedding Day ·

date: _____

COMPLETED	CONFIRMED	
☐	☐	eat a healthy breakfast
☐	☐	practice your vows
☐	☐	take a soothing bubble bath
☐	☐	spend some time alone with your parents
☐	☐	give announcements to your honor attendant to mail
☐	☐	get your hair & make-up done
☐	☐	dress
☐	☐	pose for photographs
☐	☐	enjoy your wedding!

· Rehearsal Dinner ·

Your reception dinner is a gathering for friends and close family to connect and celebrate after the rehearsal. It is customary for the groom's parents to host the event and decide who to include with the wedding party. Someone may offer to have the dinner at their home, or you may choose a restaurant near the ceremony site. This is the time to hand out copies of the wedding day itinerary to the members of your wedding party. A little speech of thanks to parents and attendants from you and your groom will be appreciated. Remember to end early enough for all to get a good night's sleep.

location: _____ time: _____

address: _____

directions: _____

_____

_____

phone: _____ e-mail: _____

contact: _____ # of guests: _____

menu: _____

_____

_____

_____

_____

_____

· Day-After Brunch ·

location: _____   time: _____

address: _____

directions: _____

_____

_____

phone: _____   e-mail: _____

contact: _____   # of guests: _____

menu: _____

_____

_____

_____

_____

_____

_____

_____

_____

_____

notes

_____

_____

_____

_____

· Ceremony Program ·

Your ceremony program should list the readings and music in order, as well as
the reader(s), performer(s), the official, and members of your wedding party.

create ceremony program here:

_____

_____

_____

_____

_____

_____

_____

_____

_____

_____

_____

_____

_____

_____

_____

_____

_____

_____

_____

_____

_____

_____

· Ceremony Program ·

paste printed program here:

Calendar

Wild carrot flowers

Queen Anne's
Lace—*virtue*
Amaranthus—
immortality, incorruptibility

Wild carrot flowers are named for the virtuous Queen Anne, the last of the Stuarts to rule England. She wore a frilly cap of lace that reminded her people of this common field flower. Anne married Prince George of Denmark and had seventeen children. During her reign in the early eighteenth century, Queen Anne established the first English public garden at Kensington Palace.

Rose, Queen Anne's Lace & Amaranthus Bouquet:

9 Lucia roses
6 stems green amaranthus
24 stems Queen Anne's lace
2 yards 3-inch-wide double-faced satin ribbon
24-gauge cloth-covered wire
light green florist tape
corsage pins

Make this bouquet the day before the wedding.

Groom the roses, removing the leaves and thorns, and wrap the stems with wire.

Cut the amaranthus tendrils off their stems. Put the cut ends together to form a loop. Twist one end of a 9-inch piece of wire around the ends and secure it with florist tape. Make approximately a dozen wired loops, and set them aside.

Make 8 clusters of Queen Anne's lace, with three flowers in each. Trim the stems to about 8 inches. Set aside.

Arrange the roses in three rows of three to form a square. Tape the stems.

Place two clusters of Queen Anne's lace on each side of the rose square. Secure with florist tape.

Arrange the wired amaranthus loops around the bouquet, tucking them just under the Queen Anne's lace, so they hang like swag fringed.

Tape the wires neatly to the stem handle. Trim the handle to a point.

Mist the bouquet well, and store in the refrigerator.

Shortly before the wedding, wrap the handle tightly with half a yard of the ribbon. Secure the ribbon in place with a corsage pin.

To finish, tie the remaining ribbon in a soft bow at the top of the handle.

Calendar

To help manage your time wisely
and stay on schedule during this hectic year, enter every appointment
in this section as soon as you make it. There is a square for each day
and room for notes and reminders. Put the name of the month you
start your organizer at the top of the page, and note the number of
months remaining in the countdown to your wedding. At the end of
the section is a page dedicated to your wedding day itinerary. You will
need to copy this for the wedding party and your key people in the
last few days of preparation.

Month: _____

MONDAY	TUESDAY	WEDNESDAY	THURSDAY

Month(s) Before the Wedding

_____

FRIDAY	SATURDAY	SUNDAY

notes

_____
_____
_____
_____
_____
_____
_____
_____
_____
_____
_____
_____
_____
_____
_____
_____
_____
_____
_____
_____
_____
_____
_____

Month: _____

MONDAY	TUESDAY	WEDNESDAY	THURSDAY

_____ Month(s) Before the Wedding

FRIDAY	SATURDAY	SUNDAY	notes

Month: _____

MONDAY	TUESDAY	WEDNESDAY	THURSDAY

_____

FRIDAY	SATURDAY	SUNDAY	notes

Month: _____

MONDAY	TUESDAY	WEDNESDAY	THURSDAY

_____ Month(s) Before the Wedding

FRIDAY	SATURDAY	SUNDAY

notes

_____

_____

_____

_____

_____

_____

_____

_____

_____

_____

_____

_____

_____

_____

_____

_____

_____

_____

_____

_____

_____

_____

_____

_____

_____

Month: _____

MONDAY	TUESDAY	WEDNESDAY	THURSDAY

Month(s) Before the Wedding

FRIDAY	SATURDAY	SUNDAY

Month:

MONDAY	TUESDAY	WEDNESDAY	THURSDAY

_____ Month(s) Before the Wedding

FRIDAY	SATURDAY	SUNDAY

Month: _____

MONDAY	TUESDAY	WEDNESDAY	THURSDAY

FRIDAY	SATURDAY	SUNDAY

notes

_____

_____

_____

_____

_____

_____

_____

_____

_____

_____

_____

_____

_____

_____

_____

_____

_____

_____

_____

_____

_____

_____

_____

Month: _____

MONDAY	TUESDAY	WEDNESDAY	THURSDAY

Month(s) Before the Wedding

_____

FRIDAY	SATURDAY	SUNDAY	notes

Month:

MONDAY	TUESDAY	WEDNESDAY	THURSDAY

Month(s) Before the Wedding

_____

FRIDAY	SATURDAY	SUNDAY

Month: _____

MONDAY	TUESDAY	WEDNESDAY	THURSDAY

_____ Month(s) Before the Wedding

FRIDAY	SATURDAY	SUNDAY

notes

_____
_____
_____
_____
_____
_____
_____
_____
_____
_____
_____
_____
_____
_____
_____
_____
_____
_____
_____
_____
_____
_____
_____
_____

Month: _____

MONDAY	TUESDAY	WEDNESDAY	THURSDAY

FRIDAY	SATURDAY	SUNDAY

notes

_____
_____
_____
_____
_____
_____
_____
_____
_____
_____
_____
_____
_____
_____
_____
_____
_____
_____
_____
_____
_____

· Wedding Day Itinerary ·

Writing an itinerary for your wedding day will ease anxiety for everyone. Make a neat timetable for all scheduled events from make-up, photo sessions, departure times, arrival times, meal service, toasts, and bouquet toss. Make copies for the vendors and each member of your wedding party.

_____

_____

_____

_____

_____

_____

_____

_____

_____

_____

_____

_____

_____

_____

_____

_____

_____

_____

_____

_____

Wedding Party

Since the Middle Ages, in the mountains of Austria

and Germany, considerate men have presented their betrothed with a bride's box. Usually oval-shaped and made of wood, the delicate boxes are painted with flowers, birds, and messages of love. The box originally was meant to hold the private possessions and personal treasures of the bride-to-be when the rest of her belongings, like she herself, became the property of her husband. Gardenias are particularly loved for their sensuous fragrance. Handle them carefully, and only by their stems, since they will bruise wherever you touch the petals. Covered and refrigerated, gardenias will stay fresh for days.

Gardenia—joy, secret love

Gardenia Bouquet:

10 gardenias
5 yards 1 1/2-inch-wide wired ribbon
24-gauge white-cloth-covered wire
white florist tape
tissue paper

This bouquet may be made early on the day before the wedding. It is not difficult make, but it is time-consuming.

Cut a 30-inch piece of ribbon. Set aside.

Cut the remaining ribbon into ten 15-inch pieces.

Cut wire into eighteen 8-inch pieces and four 18-inch pieces.

From the ten 15-inch pieces of ribbon make simple bows and attach an 8-inch piece of wire to the center of each bow.

Remove the gardenia flowers from their stems.

Using 8-inch wires, wrap the stems with wire and then tape 8 gardenias.

Wire another gardenia to an 18-inch piece of wire, and wrap with tape. Lay a bow on the wire just under the edge of the flower and tape it in place.

With another 18-inch wire, start with a bow, then add a wired gardenia, then another bow, and another wired gardenia, taping as you apply each.

Wire a gardenia to a third 18-inch wire, then add a bow, a wired gardenia, a bow, and another wired gardenia.

Finally, starting with a bow, attach four gardenias and four bows to the last 18-inch wire.

Carefully, so you do not bruise the gardenias, gather the wires together.

Place the wire with four flowers in the center and the others to the sides to make an asymmetrical bouquet.

Twist one of the wires around the others to create a handle. Trim the wires evenly. Cover the handle with a generous amount of tape.

Mist the bouquet lightly and cover with a loose plastic bag. Lay the bouquet on a shelf in the refrigerator on several pieces of wrinkled tissue paper to cushion it.

Shortly before the wedding, remove the bouquet from the refrigerator.

Bend the handle behind the flowers. To finish, double the 30-inch piece of ribbon and tie into a bow at the top of the handle.

Wedding Party

The Wedding Party section is a place for you to record all the information about the wedding attire, health and beauty appointments, and honeymoon packing list. There are also pages to record the groom's attire and a reminder list of his responsibilities.

This section is also your record of the people closest to the two of you who will stand with you and give their loving support to your marriage. Fill in their contact information and sizes and note the gift you will be giving each of them. Your attendants and groomsmen are there to help and support you. Give each one of them an itinerary, locations with directions, and a contact list. Assign the duties traditionally performed by the members of the wedding party to them. It is a good idea to review these duties with them when you invite them to be a part of your wedding, and again during the weeks before the wedding.

· Bride's Attire ·

fitting:

_____
(date/time)

fitting:

_____
(date/time)

fitting:

_____
(date/time)

DRESS

$ _____
budget

$ _____
estimate

$ _____
deposit

_____
(date paid)

$ _____
balance

_____
(date due)

$ _____
extras

$ _____
final

bridal salon/store: _____

address: _____

salesperson: _____

phone: _____ fax: _____

your dress

designer: _____

color: _____

style #: _____ size: _____

description: _____

_____

photo/sketch:

· Bride's Attire ·

accessories

PRICE	ITEM/DESCRIPTION	STORE/SOURCE	ORDERED/ARRIVED	
	headpiece		▪	▪
	veil		▪	▪
	shoes		▪	▪
	lingerie		▪	▪
			▪	▪
			▪	▪
	stockings		▪	▪
	gloves		▪	▪
	jewelry		▪	▪
	wrap		▪	▪
			▪	▪
			▪	▪
			▪	▪
			▪	▪
			▪	▪
			▪	▪

▪ *something old*:

▪ *something new*:

▪ *something borrowed*:

▪ *something blue*:

ACCESSORIES

$ _____
budget

$ _____
estimate

$ _____
total cost

· Bride's Attire ·

rehearsal dinner

- ☐ dress
- ☐ shoes
- ☐ lingerie
- ☐ accessories
- ☐ jewelry
- ☐ wrap
- ☐ _____
- ☐ _____

going-away outfit

- ☐ dress
- ☐ shoes
- ☐ lingerie
- ☐ accessories
- ☐ jewelry
- ☐ wrap
- ☐ _____
- ☐ _____

honeymoon packing list

- ☐ passport
- ☐ medication/first aid kit
- ☐ hair products
- ☐ cosmetics
- ☐ sunscreen
- ☐ camera & film
- ☐ books
- ☐ _____
- ☐ _____
- ☐ _____
- ☐ _____
- ☐ _____
- ☐ _____
- ☐ _____

- ☐ _____
- ☐ _____
- ☐ _____
- ☐ _____
- ☐ _____
- ☐ _____
- ☐ _____
- ☐ _____
- ☐ _____
- ☐ _____

· Bride ·

beauty & health

COST	TREATMENT	PROVIDER	PHONE #	APPOINTMENTS	
				PRACTICE	PRE-WEDDING
	facial			▦	▦
	manicure			▦	▦
	pedicure			▦	▦
	massage			▦	▦
	doctor			▦	▦
	dentist			▦	▦
	hair			▦	▦
	make-up artist			▦	▦
				▦	▦
				▦	▦
				▦	▦
				▦	▦
				▦	▦
				▦	▦

COST	MAKE-UP
	foundation
	eyes
	blush
	lipstick
	nail polish

$ _____
budget

$ _____
estimate

$ _____
total cost

· Groom ·

duties

- participate in the planning and budget, and in making the guest list with you and your parents.
- decide with you how finances will be managed.
- choose the best man and groomsmen, and explain their duties to them.
- arrange accommodations for out-of-town groomsmen and family.
- visit ceremony and reception sites and interview vendors with you.
- set up appointment with official and attend counseling or classes.
- help design the invitations.
- order tuxedo and attend fittings.
- choose a gift for you and each of his groomsmen.
- buy ties for groomsmen and ushers.
- order wedding rings and pick them up.
- make reservations for the wedding night and arrange transportation.
- register for gifts with you.
- get a physical and a blood test.
- see a dentist; perhaps have teeth whitened.
- apply for a marriage license with you.
- renew passport, update official records, bank accounts, credit cards, and insurance beneficiary.
- execute new will.
- help write thank-you notes.
- pay for the bridal bouquet, boutonnieres, and the mothers' flowers.
- arrange the honeymoon and pick up tickets and travelers checks.
- pack for honeymoon.
- help you design the seating chart.
- write his wedding vows and memorize them.
- pay the official (he can give the check to his best man to do this).
- spend time with each of your guests at the reception, and be sure his entire family is introduced to yours.
- dance the second dance with your mother.
- toast all the parents at the reception.
- be on time, be patient, smile.

· Groom's Attire ·

store: _____

address: _____

salesperson: _____

phone: _____ fax: _____

designer: _____

style #: _____

color: _____ size: _____

description: _____

_____

ORDERED	DELIVERED	ITEM
▨	▨	jacket: _____
		size sleeve
▨	▨	pants: _____
		waist inseam
▨	▨	shirt: _____
		neck sleeve
▨	▨	suspenders: _____
▨	▨	cummerbund: _____
▨	▨	cuff links, shirt studs: _____
▨	▨	tie, handkerchief: _____
▨	▨	socks: _____
▨	▨	shoes: _____
▨	▨	_____
▨	▨	_____
▨	▨	

fitting: _____

_____
(date/time)

fitting: _____

_____
(date/time)

fitting: _____

_____
(date/time)

delivery/pick-up: _____

_____
(date/time)

ATTIRE

$ _____
budget

$ _____
deposit

_____
(date paid)

$ _____
balance

_____
(date due)

$ _____
final cost

· Attendants ·

honor attendant's duties

- assist you in choosing your gown and attendant dresses.
- assist you in addressing invitations.
- throw the bridal shower; record shower gifts.
- make appointments for dress fittings.
- help make the wedding favors.
- schedule attendants for rehearsal.
- give a toast at the rehearsal dinner.
- assist you with dressing.
- escort you to wedding.
- bring groom's ring to ceremony.
- keep track of your make-up kit.
- adjust veil and train during ceremony and photographs.
- hold bouquet during ring exchange and vows.
- witness and sign marriage certificate.
- participate in receiving line.
- dance with the best man during bridal party dance.
- help you dress into going-away outfit.
- bring wedding gown and accessories home.
- mail announcements.

bridal attendants' duties

- assist you in addressing invitations.
- help throw the bridal shower.
- help make the wedding favors.
- make appointments for dress fittings.
- attend the rehearsal.
- attend the rehearsal dinner.
- assist you with dressing.
- escort you to wedding.
- participate in receiving line.
- dance with groomsman during bridal party dance.
- help you dress into going-away outfit.

· Attendants ·

wedding attire

store: _____

address: _____

salesperson: _____

phone: _____ fax: _____

designer: _____

color: _____ style #: _____

cost: _____

description: _____

_____

fitting: _____

(date/time)

fitting: _____

(date/time)

fitting: _____

(date/time)

delivery/pick-up: _____

(date/time)

notes & photos

· Honor Attendant ·

first fitting:

_____

(date/time)

_____

final fitting:

_____

(date/time)

name: _____

address: _____

_____

home phone: _____ work: _____

cell: _____ fax: _____

e-mail: _____

gift: _____

measurements

bust: _____ waist: _____ hips: _____

attire

ORDERED	DELIVERED	ITEM	SIZE	SOURCE/STORE
☐	☐	dress		
☐	☐	lingerie		
☐	☐			
☐	☐	gloves		
☐	☐	hat		
☐	☐	shoes		
☐	☐	jewelry		
☐	☐	wrap		
☐	☐	stockings		

notes

· Bridal Attendants ·

name: _____

address: _____

_____

home phone: _____ work: _____

cell: _____ fax: _____

e-mail: _____

gift: _____

first fitting:

_____

(date/time)

final fitting:

_____

(date/time)

measurements

bust: _____ waist: _____ hips: _____

attire

ORDERED	DELIVERED	ITEM	SIZE	SOURCE/STORE
☐	☐	dress		_____
☐	☐	lingerie		_____
☐	☐			_____
☐	☐	gloves		_____
☐	☐	hat		_____
☐	☐	shoes		_____
☐	☐	jewelry		_____
☐	☐	wrap		_____
☐	☐	stockings		_____

notes

· Bridal Attendants ·

first fitting:

_____

(*date/time*)

_____

final fitting:

_____

(*date/time*)

name: _____

address: _____

_____

home phone: _____ work: _____

cell: _____ fax: _____

e-mail: _____

gift: _____

measurements

bust: _____ waist: _____ hips: _____

attire

ORDERED	DELIVERED	ITEM	SIZE	SOURCE/STORE
☐	☐	dress		
☐	☐	lingerie		
☐	☐			
☐	☐	gloves		
☐	☐	hat		
☐	☐	shoes		
☐	☐	jewelry		
☐	☐	wrap		
☐	☐	stockings		

notes

· Bridal Attendants ·

name: _____

address: _____

_____

home phone: _____ work: _____

cell: _____ fax: _____

e-mail: _____

gift: _____

first fitting:

_____

(date/time)

final fitting:

_____

(date/time)

measurements

bust: _____ waist: _____ hips: _____

attire

ORDERED	DELIVERED	ITEM	SIZE	SOURCE/STORE
☐	☐	dress		
☐	☐	lingerie		
☐	☐			
☐	☐	gloves		
☐	☐	hat		
☐	☐	shoes		
☐	☐	jewelry		
☐	☐	wrap		
☐	☐	stockings		

notes

· Bridal Attendants ·

first fitting:

_____

(date/time)

final fitting:

_____

(date/time)

name: _____

address: _____

_____

home phone: _____ work: _____

cell: _____ fax: _____

e-mail: _____

gift: _____

measurements

bust: _____ waist: _____ hips: _____

attire

ORDERED	DELIVERED	ITEM	SIZE	SOURCE/STORE
☐	☐	dress		
☐	☐	lingerie		
☐	☐			
☐	☐	gloves		
☐	☐	hat		
☐	☐	shoes		
☐	☐	jewelry		
☐	☐	wrap		
☐	☐	stockings		

notes

· Bridal Attendants ·

name: _____

address: _____

_____

home phone: _____ work: _____

cell: _____ fax: _____

e-mail: _____

gift: _____

first fitting:

_____

(date/time)

_____

final fitting:

_____

(date/time)

measurements

bust: _____ waist: _____ hips: _____

attire

ORDERED	DELIVERED	ITEM	SIZE	SOURCE/STORE
☐	☐	dress		
☐	☐	lingerie		
☐	☐			
☐	☐	gloves		
☐	☐	hat		
☐	☐	shoes		
☐	☐	jewelry		
☐	☐	wrap		
☐	☐	stockings		

notes

· Bridal Attendants ·

first fitting:

_____
(date/time)

final fitting:

_____
(date/time)

name: _____

address: _____

_____

home phone: _____ work: _____

cell: _____ fax: _____

e-mail: _____

gift: _____

measurements

bust: _____ waist: _____ hips: _____

attire

ORDERED	DELIVERED	ITEM	SIZE	SOURCE/STORE
▪	▪	dress		
▪	▪	lingerie		
▪	▪			
▪	▪	gloves		
▪	▪	hat		
▪	▪	shoes		
▪	▪	jewelry		
▪	▪	wrap		
▪	▪	stockings		

notes

· Bridal Attendants ·

name: _____

address: _____

_____

home phone: _____ work: _____

cell: _____ fax: _____

e-mail: _____

gift: _____

first fitting:

_____

(date/time)

final fitting:

_____

(date/time)

measurements

bust: _____ waist: _____ hips: _____

attire

ORDERED	DELIVERED	ITEM	SIZE	SOURCE/STORE
☐	☐	dress		
☐	☐	lingerie		
☐	☐			
☐	☐	gloves		
☐	☐	hat		
☐	☐	shoes		
☐	☐	jewelry		
☐	☐	wrap		
☐	☐	stockings		

notes

· Flower Girls ·

first fitting:

_____

(date/time)

_____

final fitting:

_____

(date/time)

name: _____

address: _____

_____

home phone: _____ mom's work: _____

cell: _____ fax: _____

e-mail: _____

gift: _____

a t t i r e

ORDERED	DELIVERED	ITEM	SIZE	SOURCE/STORE
☐	☐	dress		
☐	☐	slip		
☐	☐	lingerie/underwear		
☐	☐	stockings		
☐	☐	shoes		
☐	☐	jewelry		
☐	☐	hat/head piece		
☐	☐	gloves		
☐	☐			

n o t e s

· Flower Girls ·

name: _____

address: _____

_____

home phone: _____ mom's work: _____

cell: _____ fax: _____

e-mail: _____

gift: _____

first fitting:

_____

(date/time)

_____

final fitting:

_____

(date/time)

attire

ORDERED	DELIVERED	ITEM	SIZE	SOURCE/STORE
☐	☐	dress		
☐	☐	slip		
☐	☐	lingerie/underwear		
☐	☐	stockings		
☐	☐	shoes		
☐	☐	jewelry		
☐	☐	hat/head piece		
☐	☐	gloves		
☐	☐			

notes

· Groomsmen ·

best man's duties

- organize the bachelor party.
- attend fittings for formal wear.
- schedule groomsmen/ushers for rehearsal.
- give toast at rehearsal dinner.
- assist the groom dressing.
- hold the bride's wedding ring.
- bring the marriage license to ceremony.
- drive the groom to the ceremony (on time!).
- witness and sign marriage certificate.
- pay the official.
- may drive bride and groom to reception.
- offer toast at reception.
- dance with maid of honor during wedding party dance.
- distribute checks to vendors.
- supervise packing and timely departure of the getaway car.
- organize tuxedo returns.

Groomsmen/ushers' duties

- attend all fittings, pick up and return rented attire.
- assist best man with the bachelor party.
- attend rehearsal and rehearsal dinner.
- be available for wedding photographs.
- arrive properly dressed one hour before the ceremony.
- distribute wedding programs.
- be aware of any special ceremony seating and special needs of guests.
- escort guests to their seats at ceremony; take the right arm of women guests, seat bride's guests on the left of the aisle; groom's on the right.
- escort groom's mother to her seat; the bride's mother is seated last.
- roll out the aisle runner, close door.
- take place beside the groom.
- escort bridal attendant down the aisle after ceremony, return to help guests with special needs.
- give directions to reception site.
- transport bridal attendants to reception.
- dance with attendants and guests.
- decorate the getaway car.

· Groomsmen ·

wedding attire

store: _____

address: _____

salesperson: _____

phone: _____ fax: _____

designer: _____

color: _____ style #: _____

fitting:

_____

(date/time)

fitting:

_____

(date/time)

delivery/pick-up:

_____

(date/time)

description/color   cost

jacket & pants: _____

shirt: _____

suspenders/cummerbund: _____

cuff links, shirt studs: _____

tie, handkerchief: _____

socks: _____

shoes: _____

_____

notes

· Best Man ·

fitting:

_____
(date/time)

fitting:

_____
(date/time)

delivery/pick-up:

_____
(date/time)

name: _____

address: _____

_____

home phone: _____ work: _____

cell: _____ fax: _____

e-mail: _____

gift: _____

attire

ORDERED	DELIVERED	ITEM
☐	☐	jacket: _____
		size sleeve
☐	☐	pants: _____
		waist inseam
☐	☐	shirt: _____
		neck sleeve
☐	☐	shoe: _____
		size
☐	☐	accessories: _____
		_____

notes

· Groomsmen & Ushers ·

name: _____

address: _____

home phone: _____ work: _____

cell: _____ fax: _____

e-mail: _____

a t t i r e

ORDERED	DELIVERED	ITEM	MEASUREMENTS
☐	☐	jacket:	_____
☐	☐	pants:	_____
☐	☐	shirt	_____
☐	☐	accessories/shoe size:	_____

name: _____

address: _____

home phone: _____ work: _____

cell: _____ fax: _____

e-mail: _____

first fitting:

_____

(date/time)

final fitting:

_____

(date/time)

a t t i r e

ORDERED	DELIVERED	ITEM	MEASUREMENTS
☐	☐	jacket:	_____
☐	☐	pants:	_____
☐	☐	shirt	_____
☐	☐	accessories/shoe size:	_____

· Groomsmen & Ushers ·

name: _____

address: _____

home phone: _____ work: _____

cell: _____ fax: _____

e-mail: _____

first fitting:

_____

(date/time)

final fitting:

_____

(date/time)

a t t i r e

ORDERED	DELIVERED	ITEM	MEASUREMENTS
☐	☐	jacket:	
☐	☐	pants:	
☐	☐	shirt	
☐	☐	accessories/shoe size:	

name: _____

address: _____

home phone: _____ work: _____

cell: _____ fax: _____

e-mail: _____

first fitting:

_____

(date/time)

final fitting:

_____

(date/time)

a t t i r e

ORDERED	DELIVERED	ITEM	MEASUREMENTS
☐	☐	jacket:	
☐	☐	pants:	
☐	☐	shirt	
☐	☐	accessories/shoe size:	

· Ring Bearer ·

name: _____

address: _____

_____

home phone: _____ mom's work: _____

cell: _____ fax: _____

e-mail: _____

gift: _____

ORDERED	DELIVERED	ITEM
▢	▢	jacket: _____
		size sleeve
▢	▢	pants: _____
		waist inseam
▢	▢	shirt: _____
		neck sleeve
▢	▢	suspenders
▢	▢	cummerbund
▢	▢	cuff links, shirt studs
▢	▢	tie, handkerchief
▢	▢	socks
▢	▢	shoes
▢	▢	_____
▢	▢	_____

notes

· Parents ·

Your mother should help you with all the plans. Your mother and father traditionally pay for the wedding and reception. Your mother should accompany you to choose your dress and help select the locations. Your parents should be included in compiling the guest list and selecting the menu and beverages. The bride's mother is the last to be seated, signaling the beginning of the ceremony. Usually you are escorted to the wedding and down the aisle by your father (or both parents). You dance the second dance with your father, while your groom dances with your mother. Both of your parents act as hosts at the reception, and one makes the first toast—to welcome the guests.

bride's mother

name(s): _____

address: _____

_____

home phone: _____ work: _____

cell: _____ fax: _____ e-mail: _____

wedding attire: _____

_____

bride's father

name(s): _____

address: _____

_____

home phone: _____ work: _____

cell: _____ fax: _____ e-mail: _____

wedding attire: _____

_____

· Parents ·

The groom's parents participate in making the guest list, and these days will often offer to pay some of the expense of the invitations and the reception. They should arrange accommodations for out-of-town guests invited by the groom. The rehearsal dinner is traditionally hosted and paid for by the groom's parents, and it is the groom's father who toasts the bride.

groom's mother

name(s): _____

address: _____

_____

home phone: _____ work: _____

cell: _____ fax: _____ e-mail: _____

wedding attire: _____

_____

groom's father

name(s): _____

address: _____

_____

home phone: _____ work: _____

cell: _____ fax: _____ e-mail: _____

wedding attire: _____

_____

notes

· Notes ·

Key People

In ancient times

brides carried fragrant and flowering herbs for protection from jealous evil spirits, and to guard against the threat of trolls. An herb bouquet was held to ensure the couple would enjoy good fortune, happiness, and many children.

Basil—*good wishes, serious intentions*
Bay—*glory*
Chamomile—*comfort, gentleness, sweetness*
Lavender—*devotion, luck, loyalty*
Oregano—*happiness, joy*
Rosemary—*remembrance, fidelity, constancy*
Sage—*wisdom, longevity*
Savory—*interest*
Thyme—*courage, enjoyment*

Elizabethan brides carried small bunches of fragrant dill and lavender and marigolds washed in rosewater. Europeans still include herbs in their marriage rituals. The German mother of the bride may put dill and salt in her daughter's shoe. A Czech maid of honor weaves a bridal crown of rosemary, while a bridesmaid makes a small bouquet of rosemary and pins it on the lapel of the single man she wishes will escort her to the wedding. In France bay laurel leaves are scattered on the path from the church.

Herb Bouquet:

8 clusters basil
18 stems lavender (2 varieties)
8 stems winter savory
30-40 German chamomile flowers
8 stems flowering thyme
5 stems flowering oregano
5 stems culinary oregano
4 stems Ladies Mantle
5 stems rosemary
8 stems wood sage
3 stems lemon balm
2 sprigs bay laurel
1 yard 1 1/2-inch wide linen ribbon
Green florist tape, 24-gauge cloth-covered wire,
cotton balls, plastic wrap

Making this bouquet requires a lot of time, so make it the day before the wedding. Groom the herbs, removing brown or bruised leaves and flowers; clean the stems. Using the herbs with the shortest stems—sage, basil, the smallest of the lavender stems, savory, chamomile flowers, and flowering thyme—make 8 small clusters of herbs layered according to their size, largest at the base, smallest on top. Snip the stems to an even length. Wrap the cut ends with a small piece of wet cotton, cover with plastic wrap, and tape the plastic onto the stems. This will keep the cut ends wet and the herbs fresh.

Gently wrap the end of each cluster with a 10-inch piece of wire. Cover the wire and the cotton with florist tape. Set clusters aside.

This bouquet is made to hold horizontally in the bride's right hand. For best results construct it while looking into a mirror, with the herbs held in *your* right hand.

Begin with the herbs that have the longest stems: culinary oregano and flowering oregano, ladies mantle, and lavender. Add them one at a time, forming a crescent. Add rosemary, wood sage, lemon balm, and bay laurel leaves. Loosely tape the stems together as you add them, forming a handle.

Tuck in the wired herb clusters close to the handle, and into the body of the bouquet—take care to fill any bare spaces. Adjust the position of each cluster as you build a plump crescent-shaped bouquet. The herbs should appear to shower from the handle. Tape the cluster wires to the handle. Clip wires and stems to equal length. Mist well; place in a plastic bag in the refrigerator overnight. Cover the handle neatly with a natural linen ribbon.

Key People

When you decide to engage vendor services, record ALL the information in this section. You never want to say, "Oh, no, I didn't write it down!" There is space for contact information, rates, budget and expenditures, deposits paid, services provided, and the terms of your agreement with them. This is your record of each vendor service from the caterer to the driver of your getaway car. A complete list of the flowers you will need, and all the rentals required are included along with space for a song list, a sketch of your cake, and a shot list for your photographer.

· Tasks ·

There are a few tasks you can assign to friends and family who want to make a meaningful contribution to the day. Assign them the following little, but essential jobs:

deliver ring pillow & unity candle to ceremony: _____

deliver & set out favors: _____

deliver toasting glasses, cake knife & server, guest book: _____

bring going-away outfit to reception site: _____

circulate guest book during reception: _____

take gifts from reception: _____

    to: _____

take wedding gown from reception: _____

    to: _____

take cake top from reception: _____

    to: _____

_____

_____

_____

notes

_____

_____

_____

_____

_____

_____

_____

· Jeweler/Coordinator ·

jeweler

name:

address:

contact:

phone: fax:

e-mail:

describe rings:

engraving:

$ _____
budget

$ _____
bride's

$ _____
groom's

$ _____
total cost

wedding coordinator

name:

address:

contact:

phone: fax:

e-mail:

terms:

$ _____
budget

$ _____
estimate

$ _____
deposit

$ _____
date paid

$ _____
balance

(date due)

$ _____
extras

$ _____
final

· Printer ·

$ _____
budget

$ _____
estimate

$ _____
deposit

_____
(date paid)

$ _____
balance

_____
(date due)

$ _____
final cost

name: _____

address: _____

_____

contact: _____

phone: _____ cell: _____

fax: _____ e-mail: _____

ordered: _____ delivery: _____

      day/time   *day/time*

date confirmed: _____ by: _____

description, colors/materials: _____

_____

_____

_____

_____

s k e t c h   d e s i g n   i d e a s   h e r e :

· Printer ·

printer

# ORDERED	DESCRIPTION	COST
	invitations	
	envelopes	
	response cards	
	envelopes	
	map/directions	
	enclosures	
	announcements	
	envelopes	
	envelopes	
	programs	
	place cards	
	thank-you notes	

invitation text here:

· Officiant/Ceremony Musicians ·

$ _____
budget

$ _____
fee

$ _____
extras

$ _____
final cost

wedding officiant

name: _____

address: _____

_____

phone: _____ cell: _____

fax: _____ e-mail: _____

classes required: _____

_____

$ _____
budget

$ _____
fee

$ _____
deposit

_____
(date paid)

$ _____
extras

$ _____
final cost

ceremony musicians

name: _____

address: _____

_____

contact: _____

phone: _____ cell: _____

fax: _____ e-mail: _____

rate: _____

time booked: _____ until: _____

ceremony selections

seating: _____

processional: _____

ceremony: _____

_____

recessional: _____

_____

· Wedding Ceremony Site ·

name:

address:

contact:

phone: cell:

fax: e-mail:

directions:

time booked: until:

rehearsal time booked: until:

terms/restrictions:

$

budget

$

estimate

$

deposit

(date paid)

$

balance

(date due)

$

extras

$

final cost

notes/sketches

· Reception Site ·

$ _____
budget

$ _____
estimate

$ _____
deposit

_____
(date paid)

$ _____
balance

_____
(date due)

$ _____
extras

$ _____
final cost

place: _____

address: _____

_____

contact: _____

phone: _____ cell: _____

fax: _____ website/e-mail: _____

directions: _____

_____

_____

time booked: _____ until: _____

terms/restrictions: _____

_____

_____

_____

_____

services provided: _____

_____

_____

_____

_____

equipment provided: _____

_____

_____

_____

_____

· Reception Site ·

notes/sketches

· Reception Musicians/DJ ·

$ _____
budget

$ _____
fee

$ _____
deposit

_____
(date paid)

$ _____
gratuity

_____
(date paid)

$ _____
final cost

name: _____

address: _____

_____

contact: _____

phone: _____ cell: _____

fax: _____ e-mail: _____

time booked: _____ until: _____

rate: _____ overtime rate: _____

reception selections

bride & groom's entrance: _____

first dance: _____

bride & father's dance: _____

last dance: _____

song list

_____   _____

_____   _____

_____   _____

_____   _____

_____   _____

_____   _____

_____   _____

_____   _____

· Parking/Security ·

parking valet

service: _____

address: _____

_____

contact: _____

phone: _____ cell: _____

fax: _____ website/e-mail: _____

time booked: _____ until: _____

terms: _____

_____

_____

_____

$ _____
budget

$ _____
fee

$ _____
deposit

$ _____
gratuity

$ _____
final cost

security

service: _____

address: _____

_____

contact: _____

phone: _____ cell: _____

fax: _____ website/e-mail: _____

time booked: _____ until: _____

terms: _____

_____

_____

$ _____
budget

$ _____
fee

$ _____
deposit

$ _____
gratuity

$ _____
final cost

· Transportation ·

$ _____
budget

$ _____
fee

$ _____
deposit

_____
(date due)

$ _____
gratuity

$ _____
final cost

name: _____

address: _____

_____

contact: _____

rates: _____

phone: _____ cell: _____

fax: _____ e-mail: _____

website: _____

description/notes: _____

_____

_____

_____

to ceremony:

_____

| DRIVER #1 | PICK-UP TIME |

location: _____

passengers: _____

_____

_____

_____

| DRIVER #2 | PICK-UP TIME |

location: _____

passengers: _____

_____

_____

· Transportation ·

to reception: _____

	DRIVER #1	PICK-UP TIME

location: _____

passengers: _____

_____

_____

	DRIVER #2	PICK-UP TIME

location: _____

passengers: _____

_____

_____

from reception: _____

	DRIVER #1	PICK-UP TIME

location: _____

passengers: _____

_____

_____

	DRIVER #2	PICK-UP TIME

location: _____

passengers: _____

_____

_____

· Caterer ·

$ _____
budget

$ _____
estimate

$ _____
deposit

_____
(date paid)

$ _____
balance

_____
(date due)

$ _____
extras

$ _____
final cost

company: _____

address: _____

_____

contact: _____

phone: _____ cell: _____

fax: _____ e-mail: _____

estimated # of guests: _____ final #: _____

terms: _____

_____

_____

_____

_____

_____

_____

_____

_____

notes

_____

_____

_____

_____

_____

_____

_____

· Menu ·

hors d' oeuvres   beverages   COST

_____   _____
_____   _____
_____   _____
_____   _____
_____   _____

appetizers   beverages   COST

_____   _____
_____   _____
_____   _____
_____   _____
_____   _____

entrées   beverages   COST

_____   _____
_____   _____
_____   _____
_____   _____
_____   _____

dessert   beverages   COST

_____   _____
_____   _____
_____   _____
_____   _____
_____   _____

· Rentals ·

$ _____
budget

$ _____
estimate

$ _____
deposit

_____
(date paid)

$ _____
balance

_____
(date due)

$ _____
final cost

company: _____

address: _____

_____

contact: _____

phone: _____ cell: _____

fax: _____ e-mail: _____

	DAY	**TIME**
date ordered:		
delivery:		
set-up:		
pick-up:		
date confirmed:	by:	
terms:		

notes

_____

_____

_____

_____

_____

_____

_____

_____

_____

· Rentals ·

# ORDERED	ITEM/DESCRIPTION	COST
ceremony		
	arch/chuppah	
	chairs	
	aisle runner	
	other	
reception		
	tent	
	lighting	
	heaters	
	dance floor	
	guest tables	
	serving tables	
	chairs	
	coolers	
	trash cans	

· Rentals ·

# ORDERED	ITEM/DESCRIPTION	COST

table service

	knives	
	forks	
	spoons	
	champagne glasses	
	wine glasses	
	water glasses	
	hors d' oeuvre plates	
	bread & butter plates	
	dinner plates	
	dessert plates	
	napkins	
	table linen	
	other	

notes

· Florist ·

$ _____
budget

$ _____
estimate

$ _____
deposit

_____
(date paid)

$ _____
balance

_____
(date due)

$ _____
final cost

name: _____

address: _____

_____

contact: _____

phone: _____ cell: _____

fax: _____ e-mail: _____

date ordered: _____

delivery: _____

set-up: _____

pick-up: _____

date confirmed: _____ by: _____

n o t e s

_____

_____

_____

_____

_____

_____

_____

_____

· Flowers ·

#	DESCRIPTION	COST
wedding party		
	bridal bouquet	
	toss bouquet	
	bridal headpiece	
	honor attendant bouquet	
	bridal attendant bouquets	
	flower girl(s)	
	attendants' headpieces	
	mothers' flowers	
	mothers' flowers	
	grandmothers' flowers	
boutonnieres		
	groom	
	best man & groomsmen	
	fathers & others	
	ushers	

· Flowers ·

#	DESCRIPTION	COST
ceremony		
	chuppah/archway	
	pew decorations	
	entry flowers	
	altar arrangements	
reception		
	centerpieces	
	bride's table	
	buffet table	
	entry	
	guest book table	
	powder room	

· Baker ·

name: _____

address: _____

_____

contact: _____

phone: _____ cell: _____

fax: _____ e-mail: _____

ordered: _____ delivery: _____

day/time *day/time*

set-up: _____

servings: _____ cake top: _____

description: _____

_____

_____

s k e t c h   c a k e   d e s i g n   h e r e :

$ _____
budget

$ _____
estimate

$ _____
deposit

_____
(date paid)

$ _____
balance

_____
(date due)

$ _____
groom's cake

$ _____
cake top

$ _____
final cost

· Calligrapher ·

name: _____

address: _____

_____

contact: _____

phone: _____ cell: _____

fax: _____ e-mail: _____

$ _____

budget

$ _____

estimate

$ _____

deposit

_____

(date paid)

$ _____

balance

_____

(date due)

$ _____

final cost

invitations

ordered: _____ delivery: _____

day/time *day/time*

date confirmed: _____ by: _____

place cards

ordered: _____ delivery: _____

day/time *day/time*

date confirmed: _____ by: _____

notes

_____

_____

_____

_____

_____

_____

_____

_____

_____

· Videographer ·

$ _____
budget

$ _____
estimate

$ _____
deposit

_____
(date paid)

$ _____
balance

_____
(date due)

$ _____
final cost

name: _____

address: _____

_____

contact: _____

phone: _____   cell: _____

fax: _____   e-mail: _____

time booked: _____   until: _____

date confirmed: _____   by: _____

terms: _____

_____

_____

_____

_____

notes

_____

_____

_____

_____

_____

_____

_____

_____

_____

· Photographer ·

name:

address:

contact:

phone: cell:

fax: e-mail:

wedding rate:

time booked: until:

date confirmed: by:

portrait appointment date & time:

terms:

$

budget

$

estimate

$

deposit

(date paid)

$

balance

(date due)

$

final cost

s h o t   l i s t

· Travel Agent ·

agency

name: _____

address: _____

_____

agent: _____

phone: _____ cell: _____

fax: _____ e-mail: _____

date confirmed: _____ by: _____

notes

_____

_____

_____

_____

$ _____

budget

$ _____

deposit

_____

(date paid)

$ _____

balance

_____

(date due)

$ _____

final cost

wedding night

destination: _____

_____

_____

_____

transportation: _____

_____

_____

_____

· Honeymoon ·

itinerary

depart: _____

          day/date   *airline*   *flight #*   *time*

arrive: _____

          day/date   *airline*   *flight #*   *time*

transportation: _____

destination: _____

_____

depart: _____

          day/date   *airline*   *flight #*   *time*

arrive: _____

          day/date   *airline*   *flight #*   *time*

transportation: _____

destination: _____

_____

requirements

- [ ] *passport* _____
- [ ] *visa(s):* _____
- [ ] *innoculations:* _____

notes

_____

_____

_____

$ _____

budget

$ _____

tickets:

$ _____

accommodations:

$ _____

other:

$ _____

final:

· Honeymoon ·

notes

_____

_____

_____

_____

_____

_____

_____

_____

_____

_____

_____

_____

_____

_____

_____

_____

_____

_____

_____

_____

_____

_____

Guests

At a Polish wedding, sugar is sprinkled on the bouquet to keep the bride sweet-tempered.

Pink Rose—
perfect happiness

Pink Rose Bouquet:

15 medium roses
36 stems miniature roses
1 yard 1 1/2-inch-wide decorative-edged ribbon
floral foam bouquet holder with slanted handle*

Make this bouquet the day before the wedding.

Soak the bouquet holder in cool water until no air bubbles appear.

Groom the medium roses, removing the leaves and thorns. Cut the stems to 2 1/2 inches.

Put the bouquet holder into a heavy container so you can use both hands to apply the flowers.

Arrange the medium roses around the edge of the holder by pushing the stems into the foam, the flowers facing away from the center. Place the most pointed rose at the bottom to make the point of the heart shape. Leave a space in the center of the top to make the indentation of the heart.

Groom the miniature roses, leaving a few buds and tiny leaves. Cut the stems to 1 1/2 inches.

Push the stems of the miniature roses into the foam, filling in the heart and completely covering the foam.

Mist the bouquet lightly, cover with a loose plastic bag, and keep in a cool place.

Shortly before the wedding, double the ribbon and tie a bow on the top of the handle.

To finish, pull the loops toward the bottom of the bouquet.

* *easily found in crafts and florist supply stores*

Guests

Your guests are the community that provides a supportive environment and bears witness to your commitment. Give them every courtesy, plenty of notice before your day, a welcoming atmosphere, an excellent meal, and help with accommodations and transportation—for a destination wedding or for your out-of-town guests.

The guest list can be an unwieldy mess if you let it get out of hand. In the beginning the two of you—with your families—should make a list of everyone who would be invited if space and money were not factors. Pare it down to the number you have decided on next. Live with the list until your invitations are printed, making additions and changes as they come up. Have a meeting to make the final list, then record those names and addresses in the Guests section. Note responses, the number in each party, seating, accommodations, and gift as soon as you receive them.

You will want to make a copy of the guest list on your computer for the calligrapher and the security service. You also need copies for the parents and members of the wedding party so they may familiarize themselves with the names of the guests.

· Gift Registry ·

	PATTERN	MANUFACTURER	STYLE #
china			
silver			
crystal			
cookware			

stores

	NAME	LOCATION	WEBSITE

notes

· Guest List ·

guest(s): _____

address: _____

phone: _____ e-mail: _____

accommodations: _____

gift: _____

☐ rsvp   # attending:_____   table #: _____   ☐ thank you sent

guest(s): _____

address: _____

phone: _____ e-mail: _____

accommodations: _____

gift: _____

☐ rsvp   # attending:_____   table #: _____   ☐ thank you sent

guest(s): _____

address: _____

phone: _____ e-mail: _____

accommodations: _____

gift: _____

☐ rsvp   # attending:_____   table #: _____   ☐ thank you sent

guest(s): _____

address: _____

phone: _____ e-mail: _____

accommodations: _____

gift: _____

☐ rsvp   # attending:_____   table #: _____   ☐ thank you sent

· Guest List ·

guest(s): _____

address: _____

phone: _____ e-mail: _____

accommodations: _____

gift: _____

⬛ rsvp   # attending:_____   table #: _____   ⬛ thank you sent

guest(s): _____

address: _____

phone: _____ e-mail: _____

accommodations: _____

gift: _____

⬛ rsvp   # attending:_____   table #: _____   ⬛ thank you sent

guest(s): _____

address: _____

phone: _____ e-mail: _____

accommodations: _____

gift: _____

⬛ rsvp   # attending:_____   table #: _____   ⬛ thank you sent

guest(s): _____

address: _____

phone: _____ e-mail: _____

accommodations: _____

gift: _____

⬛ rsvp   # attending:_____   table #: _____   ⬛ thank you sent

· Guest List ·

guest(s): _____

address: _____

phone: _____ e-mail: _____

accommodations: _____

gift: _____

▦ rsvp   # attending: _____ table #: _____ ▦ thank you sent

guest(s): _____

address: _____

phone: _____ e-mail: _____

accommodations: _____

gift: _____

▦ rsvp   # attending: _____ table #: _____ ▦ thank you sent

guest(s): _____

address: _____

phone: _____ e-mail: _____

accommodations: _____

gift: _____

▦ rsvp   # attending: _____ table #: _____ ▦ thank you sent

guest(s): _____

address: _____

phone: _____ e-mail: _____

accommodations: _____

gift: _____

▦ rsvp   # attending: _____ table #: _____ ▦ thank you sent

· Guest List ·

guest(s): _____

address: _____

phone: _____ e-mail: _____

accommodations: _____

gift: _____

☐ rsvp   # attending:_____ table #: _____ ☐ thank you sent

guest(s): _____

address: _____

phone: _____ e-mail: _____

accommodations: _____

gift: _____

☐ rsvp   # attending:_____ table #: _____ ☐ thank you sent

guest(s): _____

address: _____

phone: _____ e-mail: _____

accommodations: _____

gift: _____

☐ rsvp   # attending:_____ table #: _____ ☐ thank you sent

guest(s): _____

address: _____

phone: _____ e-mail: _____

accommodations: _____

gift: _____

☐ rsvp   # attending:_____ table #: _____ ☐ thank you sent

· Guest List ·

guest(s): _____

address: _____

phone: _____ e-mail: _____

accommodations: _____

gift: _____

■ rsvp   # attending: _____   table #: _____   ■ thank you sent

guest(s): _____

address: _____

phone: _____ e-mail: _____

accommodations: _____

gift: _____

■ rsvp   # attending: _____   table #: _____   ■ thank you sent

guest(s): _____

address: _____

phone: _____ e-mail: _____

accommodations: _____

gift: _____

■ rsvp   # attending: _____   table #: _____   ■ thank you sent

guest(s): _____

address: _____

phone: _____ e-mail: _____

accommodations: _____

gift: _____

■ rsvp   # attending: _____   table #: _____   ■ thank you sent

· Guest List ·

guest(s): _____

address: _____

phone: _____ e-mail: _____

accommodations: _____

gift: _____

◼ rsvp   # attending: _____   table #: _____   ◼ thank you sent

guest(s): _____

address: _____

phone: _____ e-mail: _____

accommodations: _____

gift: _____

◼ rsvp   # attending: _____   table #: _____   ◼ thank you sent

guest(s): _____

address: _____

phone: _____ e-mail: _____

accommodations: _____

gift: _____

◼ rsvp   # attending: _____   table #: _____   ◼ thank you sent

guest(s): _____

address: _____

phone: _____ e-mail: _____

accommodations: _____

gift: _____

◼ rsvp   # attending: _____   table #: _____   ◼ thank you sent

· Guest List ·

guest(s): _____

address: _____

phone: _____ e-mail: _____

accommodations: _____

gift: _____

☐ rsvp   # attending: _____   table #: _____   ☐ thank you sent

guest(s): _____

address: _____

phone: _____ e-mail: _____

accommodations: _____

gift: _____

☐ rsvp   # attending: _____   table #: _____   ☐ thank you sent

guest(s): _____

address: _____

phone: _____ e-mail: _____

accommodations: _____

gift: _____

☐ rsvp   # attending: _____   table #: _____   ☐ thank you sent

guest(s): _____

address: _____

phone: _____ e-mail: _____

accommodations: _____

gift: _____

☐ rsvp   # attending: _____   table #: _____   ☐ thank you sent

· Guest List ·

guest(s): _____

address: _____

phone: _____ e-mail: _____

accommodations: _____

gift: _____

☐ rsvp   # attending: _____   table #: _____   ☐ thank you sent

guest(s): _____

address: _____

phone: _____ e-mail: _____

accommodations: _____

gift: _____

☐ rsvp   # attending: _____   table #: _____   ☐ thank you sent

guest(s): _____

address: _____

phone: _____ e-mail: _____

accommodations: _____

gift: _____

☐ rsvp   # attending: _____   table #: _____   ☐ thank you sent

guest(s): _____

address: _____

phone: _____ e-mail: _____

accommodations: _____

gift: _____

☐ rsvp   # attending: _____   table #: _____   ☐ thank you sent

· Guest List ·

guest(s): _____

address: _____

phone: _____ e-mail: _____

accommodations: _____

gift: _____

☐ rsvp   # attending: _____   table #: _____   ☐ thank you sent

guest(s): _____

address: _____

phone: _____ e-mail: _____

accommodations: _____

gift: _____

☐ rsvp   # attending: _____   table #: _____   ☐ thank you sent

guest(s): _____

address: _____

phone: _____ e-mail: _____

accommodations: _____

gift: _____

☐ rsvp   # attending: _____   table #: _____   ☐ thank you sent

guest(s): _____

address: _____

phone: _____ e-mail: _____

accommodations: _____

gift: _____

☐ rsvp   # attending: _____   table #: _____   ☐ thank you sent

· Guest List ·

guest(s): _____

address: _____

phone: _____ e-mail: _____

accommodations: _____

gift: _____

■ rsvp   # attending: _____   table #: _____   ■ thank you sent

guest(s): _____

address: _____

phone: _____ e-mail: _____

accommodations: _____

gift: _____

■ rsvp   # attending: _____   table #: _____   ■ thank you sent

guest(s): _____

address: _____

phone: _____ e-mail: _____

accommodations: _____

gift: _____

■ rsvp   # attending: _____   table #: _____   ■ thank you sent

guest(s): _____

address: _____

phone: _____ e-mail: _____

accommodations: _____

gift: _____

■ rsvp   # attending: _____   table #: _____   ■ thank you sent

· Guest List ·

guest(s): _____

address: _____

phone: _____ e-mail: _____

accommodations: _____

gift: _____

■ rsvp   # attending: _____   table #: _____   ■ thank you sent

guest(s): _____

address: _____

phone: _____ e-mail: _____

accommodations: _____

gift: _____

■ rsvp   # attending: _____   table #: _____   ■ thank you sent

guest(s): _____

address: _____

phone: _____ e-mail: _____

accommodations: _____

gift: _____

■ rsvp   # attending: _____   table #: _____   ■ thank you sent

guest(s): _____

address: _____

phone: _____ e-mail: _____

accommodations: _____

gift: _____

■ rsvp   # attending: _____   table #: _____   ■ thank you sent

· Guest List ·

guest(s): _____

address: _____

phone: _____ e-mail: _____

accommodations: _____

gift: _____

☐ rsvp   # attending: _____ table #: _____ ☐ thank you sent

guest(s): _____

address: _____

phone: _____ e-mail: _____

accommodations: _____

gift: _____

☐ rsvp   # attending: _____ table #: _____ ☐ thank you sent

guest(s): _____

address: _____

phone: _____ e-mail: _____

accommodations: _____

gift: _____

☐ rsvp   # attending: _____ table #: _____ ☐ thank you sent

guest(s): _____

address: _____

phone: _____ e-mail: _____

accommodations: _____

gift: _____

☐ rsvp   # attending: _____ table #: _____ ☐ thank you sent

· Guest List ·

guest(s): _____

address: _____

phone: _____ e-mail: _____

accommodations: _____

gift: _____

☐ rsvp   # attending: _____ table #: _____   ☐ thank you sent

guest(s): _____

address: _____

phone: _____ e-mail: _____

accommodations: _____

gift: _____

☐ rsvp   # attending: _____ table #: _____   ☐ thank you sent

guest(s): _____

address: _____

phone: _____ e-mail: _____

accommodations: _____

gift: _____

☐ rsvp   # attending: _____ table #: _____   ☐ thank you sent

guest(s): _____

address: _____

phone: _____ e-mail: _____

accommodations: _____

gift: _____

☐ rsvp   # attending: _____ table #: _____   ☐ thank you sent

· Guest List ·

guest(s): _____

address: _____

phone: _____ e-mail: _____

accommodations: _____

gift: _____

■ rsvp   # attending:_____   table #: _____   ■ thank you sent

guest(s): _____

address: _____

phone: _____ e-mail: _____

accommodations: _____

gift: _____

■ rsvp   # attending:_____   table #: _____   ■ thank you sent

guest(s): _____

address: _____

phone: _____ e-mail: _____

accommodations: _____

gift: _____

■ rsvp   # attending:_____   table #: _____   ■ thank you sent

guest(s): _____

address: _____

phone: _____ e-mail: _____

accommodations: _____

gift: _____

■ rsvp   # attending:_____   table #: _____   ■ thank you sent

· Guest List ·

guest(s): _____

address: _____

phone: _____ e-mail: _____

accommodations: _____

gift: _____

▪ rsvp   # attending:_____   table #: _____   ▪ thank you sent

guest(s): _____

address: _____

phone: _____ e-mail: _____

accommodations: _____

gift: _____

▪ rsvp   # attending:_____   table #: _____   ▪ thank you sent

guest(s): _____

address: _____

phone: _____ e-mail: _____

accommodations: _____

gift: _____

▪ rsvp   # attending:_____   table #: _____   ▪ thank you sent

guest(s): _____

address: _____

phone: _____ e-mail: _____

accommodations: _____

gift: _____

▪ rsvp   # attending:_____   table #: _____   ▪ thank you sent

· Guest List ·

guest(s): _____

address: _____

phone: _____ e-mail: _____

accommodations: _____

gift: _____

▪ rsvp   # attending: _____ table #: _____ ▪ thank you sent

guest(s): _____

address: _____

phone: _____ e-mail: _____

accommodations: _____

gift: _____

▪ rsvp   # attending: _____ table #: _____ ▪ thank you sent

guest(s): _____

address: _____

phone: _____ e-mail: _____

accommodations: _____

gift: _____

▪ rsvp   # attending: _____ table #: _____ ▪ thank you sent

guest(s): _____

address: _____

phone: _____ e-mail: _____

accommodations: _____

gift: _____

▪ rsvp   # attending: _____ table #: _____ ▪ thank you sent

· Guest List ·

guest(s): _____

address: _____

phone: _____ e-mail: _____

accommodations: _____

gift: _____

☐ rsvp   # attending: _____ table #: _____ ☐ thank you sent

guest(s): _____

address: _____

phone: _____ e-mail: _____

accommodations: _____

gift: _____

☐ rsvp   # attending: _____ table #: _____ ☐ thank you sent

guest(s): _____

address: _____

phone: _____ e-mail: _____

accommodations: _____

gift: _____

☐ rsvp   # attending: _____ table #: _____ ☐ thank you sent

guest(s): _____

address: _____

phone: _____ e-mail: _____

accommodations: _____

gift: _____

☐ rsvp   # attending: _____ table #: _____ ☐ thank you sent

· Guest List ·

guest(s): _____

address: _____

phone: _____ e-mail: _____

accommodations: _____

gift: _____

☐ rsvp   # attending: _____ table #: _____ ☐ thank you sent

guest(s): _____

address: _____

phone: _____ e-mail: _____

accommodations: _____

gift: _____

☐ rsvp   # attending: _____ table #: _____ ☐ thank you sent

guest(s): _____

address: _____

phone: _____ e-mail: _____

accommodations: _____

gift: _____

☐ rsvp   # attending: _____ table #: _____ ☐ thank you sent

guest(s): _____

address: _____

phone: _____ e-mail: _____

accommodations: _____

gift: _____

☐ rsvp   # attending: _____ table #: _____ ☐ thank you sent

· Guest List ·

guest(s): _____

address: _____

phone: _____ e-mail: _____

accommodations: _____

gift: _____

■ rsvp   # attending: _____ table #: _____ ■ thank you sent

guest(s): _____

address: _____

phone: _____ e-mail: _____

accommodations: _____

gift: _____

■ rsvp   # attending: _____ table #: _____ ■ thank you sent

guest(s): _____

address: _____

phone: _____ e-mail: _____

accommodations: _____

gift: _____

■ rsvp   # attending: _____ table #: _____ ■ thank you sent

guest(s): _____

address: _____

phone: _____ e-mail: _____

accommodations: _____

gift: _____

■ rsvp   # attending: _____ table #: _____ ■ thank you sent

· Guest List ·

guest(s): _____

address: _____

phone: _____ e-mail: _____

accommodations: _____

gift: _____

▪ rsvp   # attending: _____ table #: _____ ▪ thank you sent

guest(s): _____

address: _____

phone: _____ e-mail: _____

accommodations: _____

gift: _____

▪ rsvp   # attending: _____ table #: _____ ▪ thank you sent

guest(s): _____

address: _____

phone: _____ e-mail: _____

accommodations: _____

gift: _____

▪ rsvp   # attending: _____ table #: _____ ▪ thank you sent

guest(s): _____

address: _____

phone: _____ e-mail: _____

accommodations: _____

gift: _____

▪ rsvp   # attending: _____ table #: _____ ▪ thank you sent

· Guest List ·

guest(s): _____

address: _____

phone: _____ e-mail: _____

accommodations: _____

gift: _____

■ rsvp   # attending: _____   table #: _____   ■ thank you sent

guest(s): _____

address: _____

phone: _____ e-mail: _____

accommodations: _____

gift: _____

■ rsvp   # attending: _____   table #: _____   ■ thank you sent

guest(s): _____

address: _____

phone: _____ e-mail: _____

accommodations: _____

gift: _____

■ rsvp   # attending: _____   table #: _____   ■ thank you sent

guest(s): _____

address: _____

phone: _____ e-mail: _____

accommodations: _____

gift: _____

■ rsvp   # attending: _____   table #: _____   ■ thank you sent

· Guest List ·

guest(s): _____

address: _____

phone: _____ e-mail: _____

accommodations: _____

gift: _____

☐ rsvp   # attending: _____   table #: _____   ☐ thank you sent

guest(s): _____

address: _____

phone: _____ e-mail: _____

accommodations: _____

gift: _____

☐ rsvp   # attending: _____   table #: _____   ☐ thank you sent

guest(s): _____

address: _____

phone: _____ e-mail: _____

accommodations: _____

gift: _____

☐ rsvp   # attending: _____   table #: _____   ☐ thank you sent

guest(s): _____

address: _____

phone: _____ e-mail: _____

accommodations: _____

gift: _____

☐ rsvp   # attending: _____   table #: _____   ☐ thank you sent

· Guest List ·

guest(s): _____

address: _____

phone: _____ e-mail: _____

accommodations: _____

gift: _____

☐ rsvp   # attending: _____ table #: _____ ☐ thank you sent

guest(s): _____

address: _____

phone: _____ e-mail: _____

accommodations: _____

gift: _____

☐ rsvp   # attending: _____ table #: _____ ☐ thank you sent

guest(s): _____

address: _____

phone: _____ e-mail: _____

accommodations: _____

gift: _____

☐ rsvp   # attending: _____ table #: _____ ☐ thank you sent

guest(s): _____

address: _____

phone: _____ e-mail: _____

accommodations: _____

gift: _____

☐ rsvp   # attending: _____ table #: _____ ☐ thank you sent

· Guest List ·

guest(s): _____

address: _____

phone: _____ e-mail: _____

accommodations: _____

gift: _____

☐ rsvp   # attending:_____   table #: _____   ☐ thank you sent

guest(s): _____

address: _____

phone: _____ e-mail: _____

accommodations: _____

gift: _____

☐ rsvp   # attending:_____   table #: _____   ☐ thank you sent

guest(s): _____

address: _____

phone: _____ e-mail: _____

accommodations: _____

gift: _____

☐ rsvp   # attending:_____   table #: _____   ☐ thank you sent

guest(s): _____

address: _____

phone: _____ e-mail: _____

accommodations: _____

gift: _____

☐ rsvp   # attending:_____   table #: _____   ☐ thank you sent

· Guest List ·

guest(s): _____

address: _____

phone: _____ e-mail: _____

accommodations: _____

gift: _____

■ rsvp   # attending: _____ table #: _____ ■ thank you sent

guest(s): _____

address: _____

phone: _____ e-mail: _____

accommodations: _____

gift: _____

■ rsvp   # attending: _____ table #: _____ ■ thank you sent

guest(s): _____

address: _____

phone: _____ e-mail: _____

accommodations: _____

gift: _____

■ rsvp   # attending: _____ table #: _____ ■ thank you sent

guest(s): _____

address: _____

phone: _____ e-mail: _____

accommodations: _____

gift: _____

■ rsvp   # attending: _____ table #: _____ ■ thank you sent

· Accommodations ·

hotel:

address:

phone: fax: website/e-mail:

guests: reservation #:   rate:

booked from: to: check out:

amenities:

directions:

reserved for:

hotel:

address:

phone: fax: website/e-mail:

guests: reservation #:   rate:

booked from: to: check out:

amenities:

directions:

reserved for:

· Accommodations ·

hotel:

address:

phone: fax: website/e-mail:

guests: reservation #:   rate:

booked from: to: check out:

amenities:

directions:

reserved for:

hotel:

address:

phone: fax: website/e-mail:

guests: reservation #:   rate:

booked from: to: check out:

amenities:

directions:

reserved for:

· Accommodations ·

hotel: _____

address: _____

_____

phone: _____ fax: _____ website/e-mail: _____

guests: _____ reservation #: _____ rate: _____

booked from: _____ to: _____ check out: _____

amenities: _____

directions: _____

_____

_____

reserved for: _____

_____

_____

hotel: _____

address: _____

_____

phone: _____ fax: _____ website/e-mail: _____

guests: _____ reservation #: _____ rate: _____

booked from: _____ to: _____ check out: _____

amenities: _____

directions: _____

_____

_____

reserved for: _____

_____

_____

Journal & Keepsakes

Anemone was the nymph cherished by gentle Zephyr, the Greek god of the west wind. The flower was created from his sweet breath and named for her. The anemone thrives in windy places and Europeans call it "wind flower" or "wind rose."

Anemone—protective love
Galyx—long-lasting
friendship

Anemone Bouquet:

16 French anemones
12 Galyx leaves
2 yards 1 1/2-inch-wide silk ribbon
green florist tape
corsage pin

This bouquet is so easy to make it can be done on the morning of the wedding or the night before.

Using scissors, trim all the leaves from the anemones.

Put the flowers into your hand one at a time in circles facing out from the center. After every four or five flowers, neatly tape the stems together forming the handle.

Arrange the galyx leaves so they are spaced evenly around the flowers. Tape the stems of the leaves to the handle.

Trim the stem handle straight across the bottom.

Place bouquet in water until an hour or two before the ceremony.

After you remove the bouquet from the water dry stems thoroughly.

Wind the ribbon around the handle tightly. Secure the ribbon at the top with a corsage pin.

To finish, tie the remaining ribbon in a fat bow at the top of handle.

Journal & Keepsakes

You think you will surely remember the little incidents that move you and make you happy during this time, but you will not remember all of them. Record these experiences —the funny and touching things people say when you tell them you are going to be married, the rush of finding the dream dress, your thoughts during the rehearsal, Dad's corny joke at the rehearsal dinner, the sweet funny encounters with family and friends. There are also pages for each of you to record the vows you will take during the ceremony. Keep this journal of your thoughts and feelings during this important time in your life. Later you will be grateful that you did. What a wonderful gift this book will be for your daughter one day.

The back pocket is for all the little treasured keepsakes you tuck away during this year—swatches, ribbon samples, a pressed boutonniere flower, the Polaroid snapshot of you trying on your dress, magazine pictures that inspired you, a sweet note from your groom. Use this section to add the personal side of the wedding year to your record of the planning and the event.

· Our Story ·

· Our Story ·

· The Proposal ·

· Our Engagement Celebration ·

· My Vows ·

· My Vows ·

· My Husband's Vows ·

_____
_____
_____
_____
_____
_____
_____
_____
_____
_____
_____
_____
_____
_____
_____
_____
_____
_____
_____
_____
_____
_____
_____
_____

· My Attendants ·

· My Attendants ·

· My Shower ·

· Journal ·

· Journal ·

· Journal ·

· Journal ·

· Journal ·

· Journal ·

Cover Bouquet

The Honor Attendant deserves a bouquet reflecting her meaningful place at the side of the bride. She is chosen to tend to the train and veil, hold the bridal bouquet while rings are given, and sign as a witness to the marriage. Married or maiden, she stands up for her sister or best friend on her wedding day.

Hydrangea—Boldness, devotion

Hydrangea Bouquet:

1 dozen white baby roses

5 or 6 blue & green hydrangeas

1 dozen crystal sprays

10 bead flowers

2 1/2 yards 1/2 inch-wide aqua wired ribbon

1 1/2 yards 3/4 inch-wide aqua sheer ribbon

Green vinyl tape,

green florist tape,

21-gauge wire

Make this bouquet the day before the wedding and keep in water.

Add the ribbons in the morning.

Clean roses of leaves and thorns and wire them. Tape a crystal spray to each rose with green florist tape. Gather the hydrangea flowers together and arrange in an oval bouquet, placing the green flowers on the bottom. Hold the bouquet in your left hand while you thread the roses and the bead flowers through the hydrangea heads throughout the bouquet.

Tape stems together, trim, and wrap with the wired ribbon. Double the remaining ribbon and tie it securely around the handle at the top. Cut ribbons to uneven lengths; curl the wired ribbons around your fingers and let them cascade down the front